EASY GUITAR
WITH NOTES & TAB

Children's Christian Songbook

T0045017

ISBN 978-0-634-01683-7

HAL•LEONARD®
CORPORATION

7777 W. BLUEMOUND RD. P.O. BOX 13819 MILWAUKEE, WI 53213

Visit Hal Leonard Online at
www.halleonard.com

STRUM AND PICK PATTERNS

This chart contains the suggested strum and pick patterns that are referred to by number at the beginning of each song in this book. The symbols ⊓ and ∨ in the strum patterns refer to down and up strokes, respectively. The letters in the pick patterns indicate which right-hand fingers plays which strings.

p = thumb
i = index finger
m = middle finger
a = ring finger

For example; Pick Pattern 2
is played: thumb - index - middle - ring

Strum Patterns

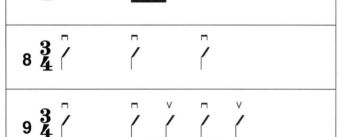

Pick Patterns

You can use the 3/4 Strum or Pick Patterns in songs written in compound meter (6/8, 9/8, 12/8, etc.). For example, you can accompany a song in 6/8 by playing the 3/4 pattern twice in each measure. The 4/4 Strum and Pick Patterns can be used for songs written in cut time (¢) by doubling the note time values in the patterns. Each pattern would therefore last two measures in cut time.

All Night, All Day

Spiritual

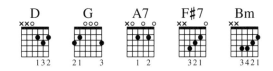

Strum Pattern: 4
Pick Pattern: 3

Verse

Moderately slow

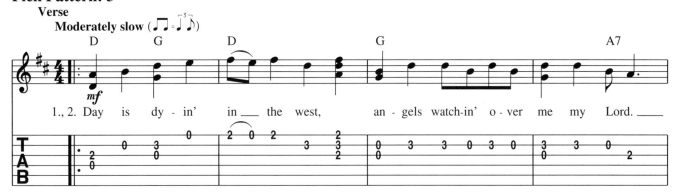

1., 2. Day is dy - in' in ___ the west, an - gels watch-in' o - ver me my Lord. ___

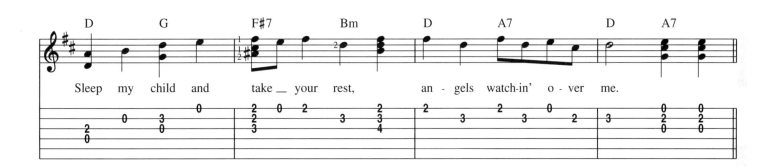

Sleep my child and take ___ your rest, an - gels watch-in' o - ver me.

Chorus

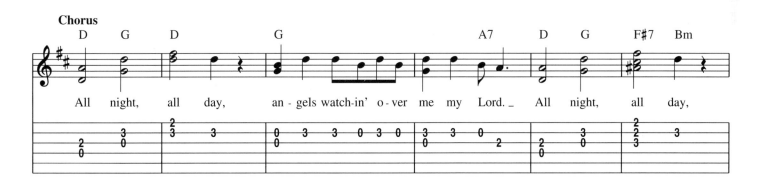

All night, all day, an - gels watch-in' o - ver me my Lord. _ All night, all day,

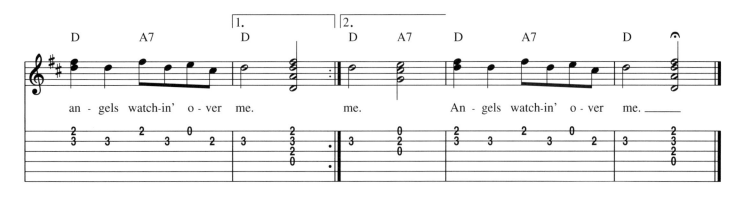

an - gels watch-in' o - ver me. me. An - gels watch-in' o - ver me. ___

Alive, Alive

Traditional

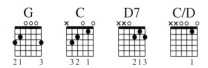

Strum Pattern: 4
Pick Pattern: 1

Verse
Moderately

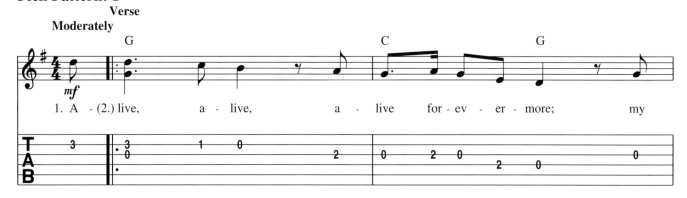

1. A - (2.) live, a - live, a - live for - ev - er - more; my

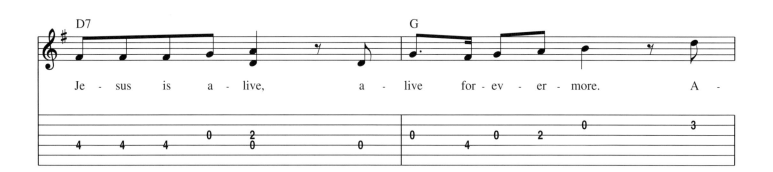

Je - sus is a - live, a - live for - ev - er - more. A -

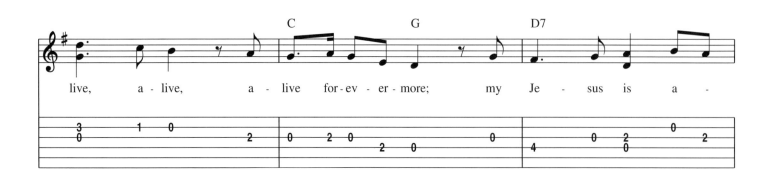

live, a - live, a - live for - ev - er - more; my Je - sus is a -

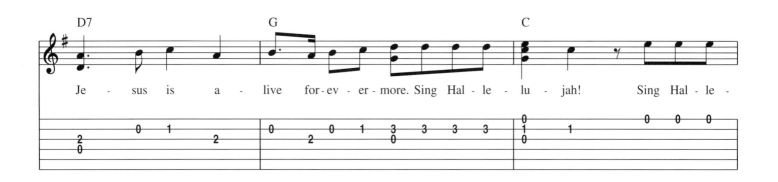

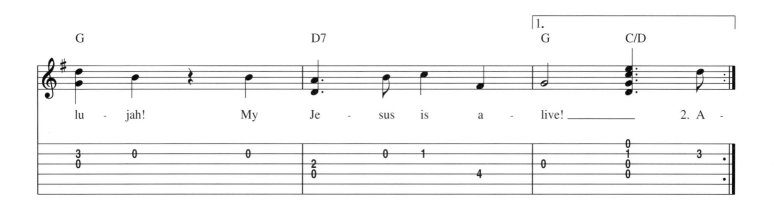

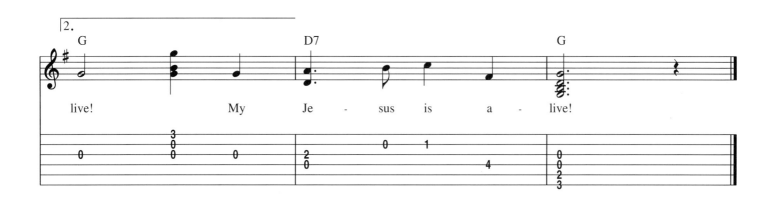

Arky, Arky

Traditional

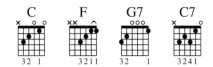

Strum Pattern: 1, 2
Pick Pattern: 2, 4

𝄋 *Verse*

Moderately

1. The Lord ___ told No - ah, there's gon - na be ___ a flood - y, flood - y,
2. - 5. *See additional lyrics*

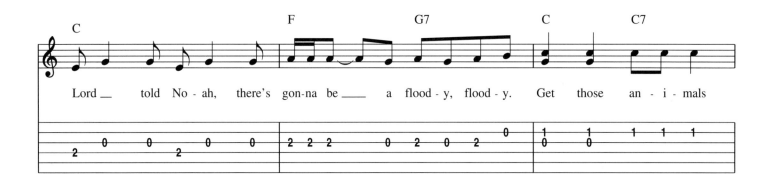

Lord ___ told No - ah, there's gon - na be ___ a flood - y, flood - y. Get those an - i - mals

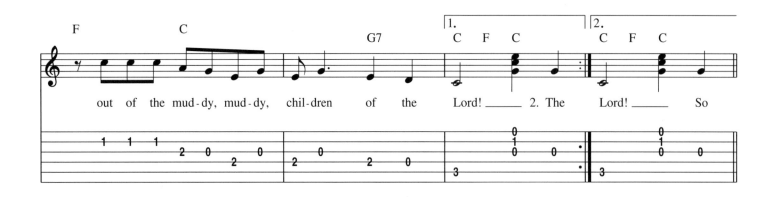

out of the mud - dy, mud - dy, chil - dren of the Lord! ___ 2. The Lord! ___ So

Chorus

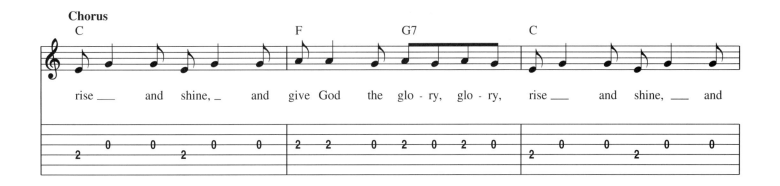

rise ___ and shine, _ and give God the glo - ry, glo - ry, rise ___ and shine, ___ and

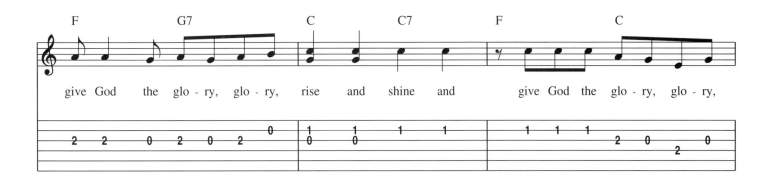

give God the glo - ry, glo - ry, rise and shine and give God the glo - ry, glo - ry,

1st time, D.S.
(take repeat)
2nd time, D.S. al Coda
(take 2nd ending)

To Coda ⊕   ⊕ **Coda**

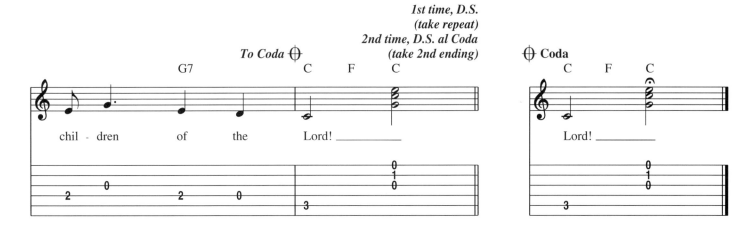

chil - dren of the Lord! _____   Lord! _____

Additional Lyrics

2. The Lord told Noah to build him an arky, arky,
   Lord told Noah to build him an arky, arky.
   Build it out of gopher barky, barky,
   Children of the Lord!

3. The animals, the animals, they came in by twosies, twosies,
   Animals, the animals, they came in by twosies, twosies.
   Elephants and kangaroosies, roosies,
   Children of the Lord!

4. It rained and poured for forty daysies, daysies,
   Rained and poured for forty daysies, daysies.
   Almost drove those animals crazies, crazies,
   Children of the Lord!

5. The sun came out and dried up the landy, landy,
   (Look there's the sun!) It dried up the landy, landy.
   Everything was fine and dandy, dandy,
   Children of the Lord!

The B-I-B-L-E

Traditional

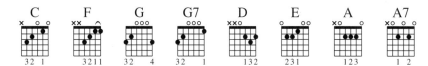

Strum Pattern: 3, 4
Pick Pattern: 3, 5

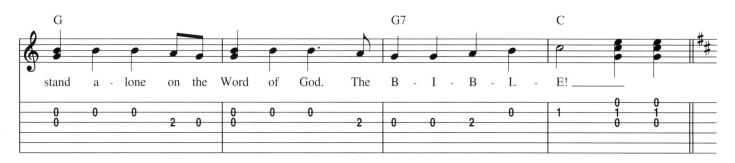

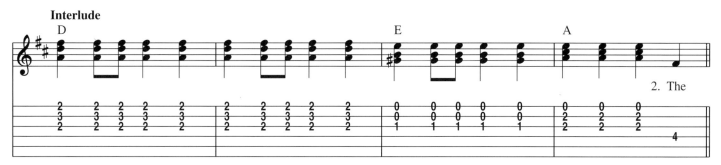

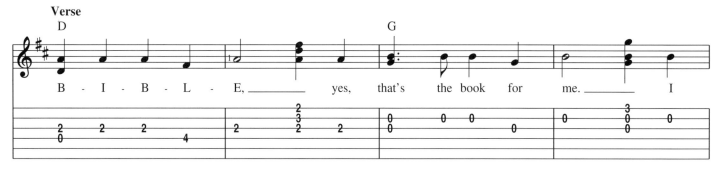

Climb, Climb Up Sunshine Mountain

Traditional

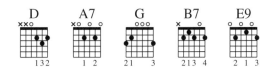

Strum Pattern: 4
Pick Pattern: 1

Verse
Moderately

1., 2. Climb, climb up Sun - shine Moun - tain, heav'n - ly breez - es blow. _____

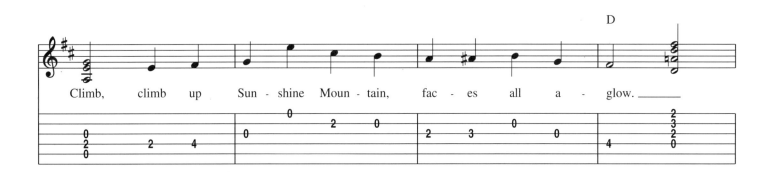

Climb, climb up Sun - shine Moun - tain, fac - es all a - glow. _____

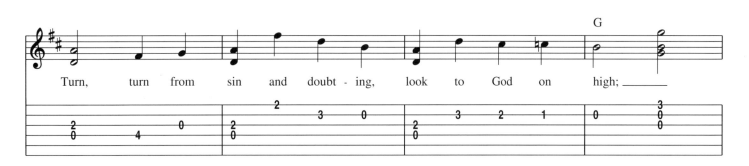

Turn, turn from sin and doubt - ing, look to God on high; _____

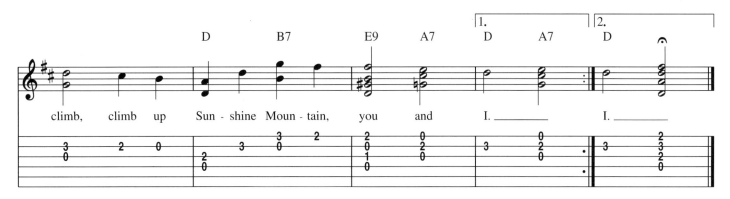

climb, climb up Sun - shine Moun - tain, you and I. _____ I. _____

Deep and Wide

Traditional

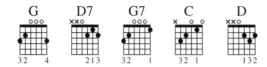

Strum Pattern: 2
Pick Pattern: 4

Intro
Moderately

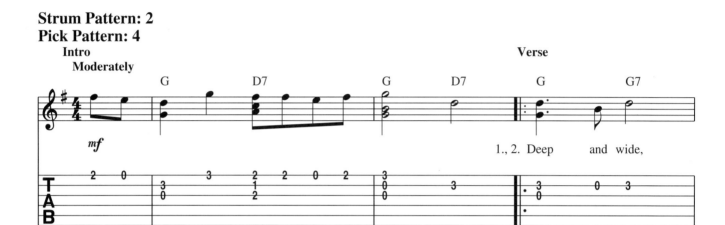

Verse

1., 2. Deep and wide,

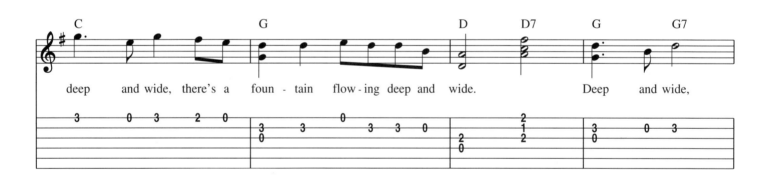

deep and wide, there's a foun - tain flow - ing deep and wide. Deep and wide,

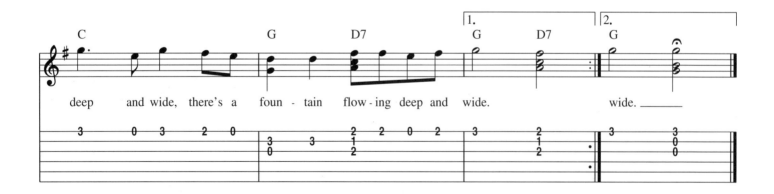

deep and wide, there's a foun - tain flow - ing deep and wide. wide. _____

Father Abraham

Traditional

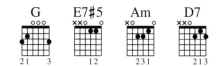

*Strum Pattern: 5
*Pick Pattern: 4

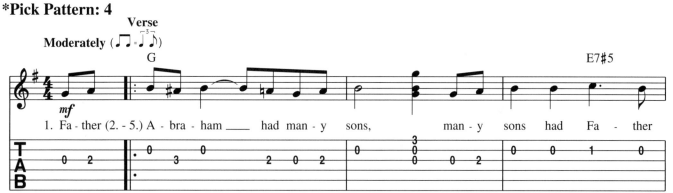

*Use Pattern 10 for 2/4 measures.

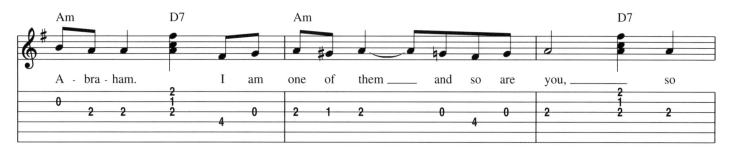

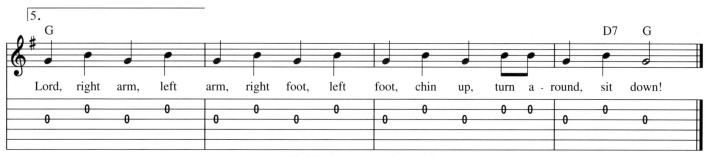

*At this point, start a continuous right arm swaying motion. Each time a new part of the body
is mentioned, that part should start a continuous motion, adding to the other motions.

Do Lord

Traditional

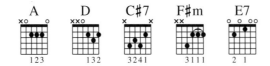

Strum Pattern: 3, 4
Pick Pattern: 1, 3

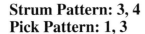

Joyfully

1. I've got a home in glo-ry land that out-shines the sun, _____
2. *See Additional Lyrics*

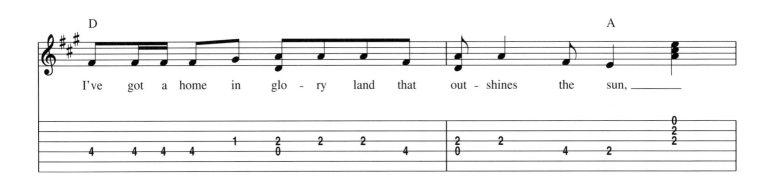

I've got a home in glo-ry land that out-shines the sun, _____

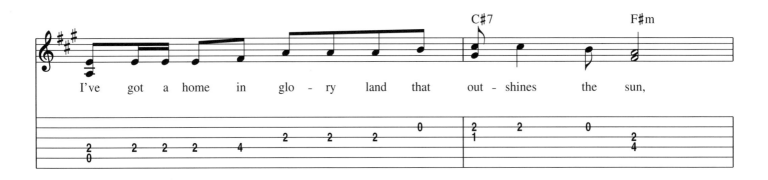

I've got a home in glo-ry land that out-shines the sun,

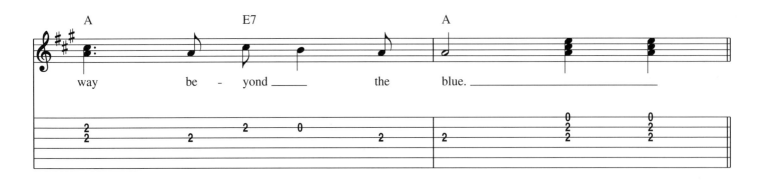

way be-yond _____ the blue. _____

Chorus

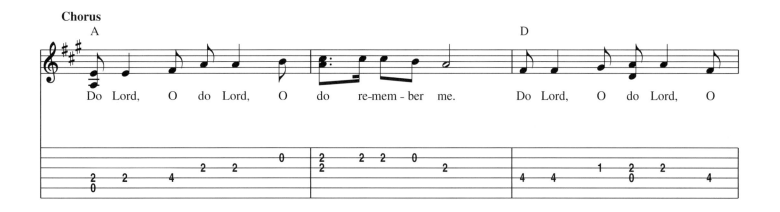

Do Lord, O do Lord, O do re-mem-ber me. Do Lord, O do Lord, O

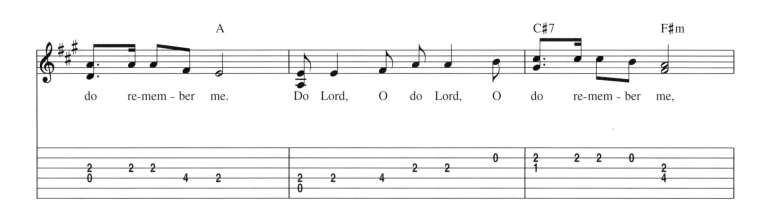

do re-mem-ber me. Do Lord, O do Lord, O do re-mem-ber me,

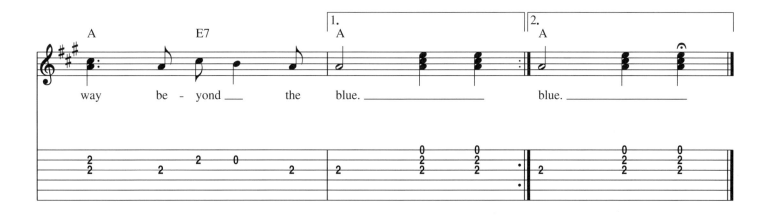

way be-yond ___ the blue. ___ blue. ___

Additional Lyrics

2. I took Jesus as my Savior; you take Him, too.
   I took Jesus as my Savior; you take Him, too.
   I took Jesus as my Savior; you take Him, too.
   While He's calling you.

Down in My Heart

Traditional

Strum Pattern: 5, 4
Pick Pattern: 1, 3

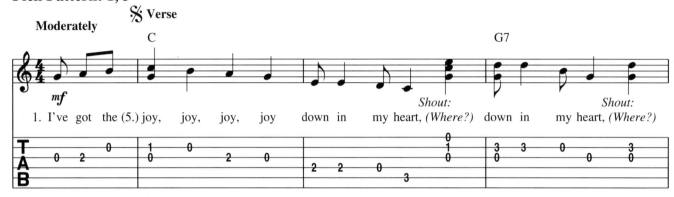

1. I've got the (5.) joy, joy, joy, joy down in my heart, *(Where?)* down in my heart, *(Where?)*

down in my heart. I've got the joy, joy, joy, joy down in my heart, *Shout:* {*(Where?)* / *(There!)*} down in my heart to

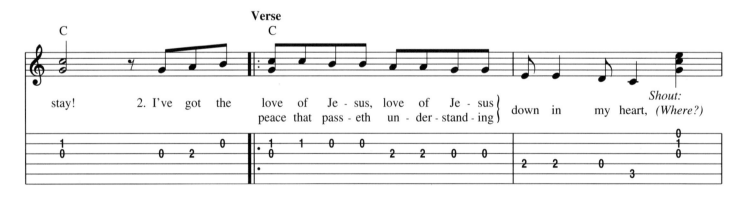

stay! 2. I've got the {love of Je - sus, love of Je - sus / peace that pass - eth un - der - stand - ing} down in my heart, *(Where?)*

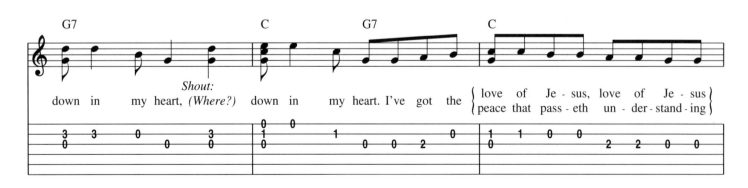

down in my heart, *(Where?)* down in my heart. I've got the {love of Je - sus, love of Je - sus / peace that pass - eth un - der - stand - ing}

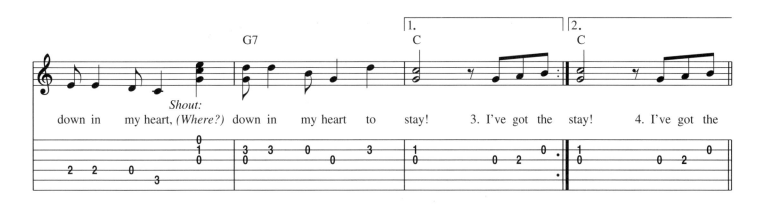

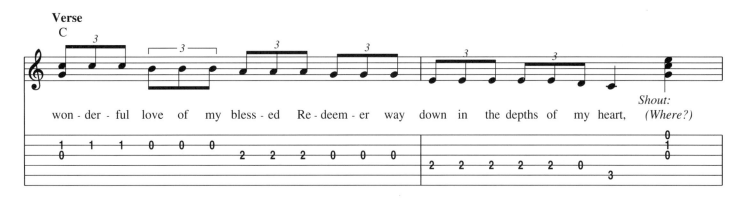

Verse

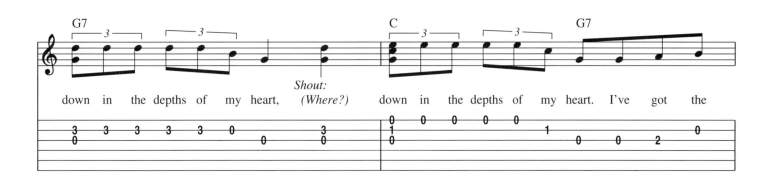

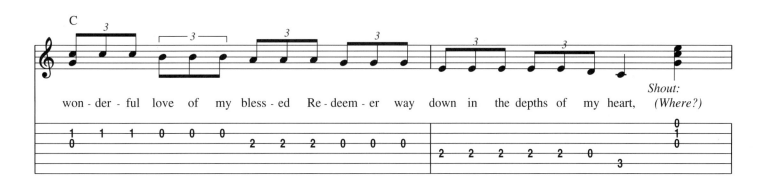

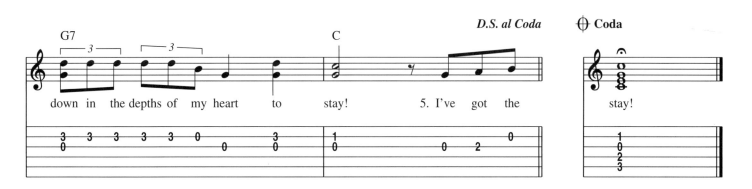

Give Me Oil in My Lamp

Traditional

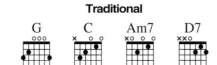

Strum Pattern: 3, 4
Pick Pattern: 1, 3

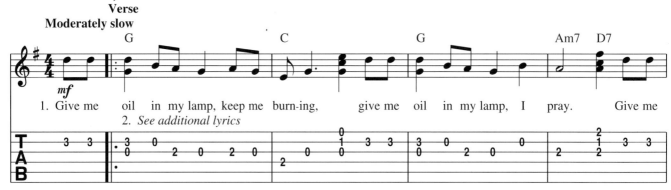

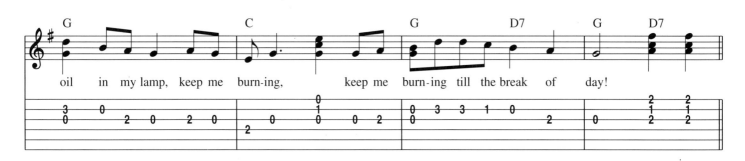

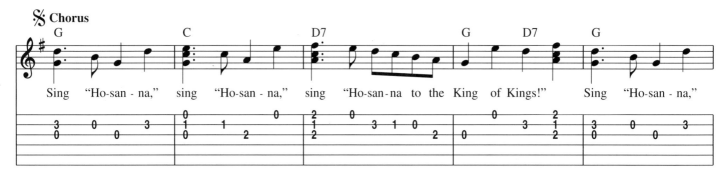

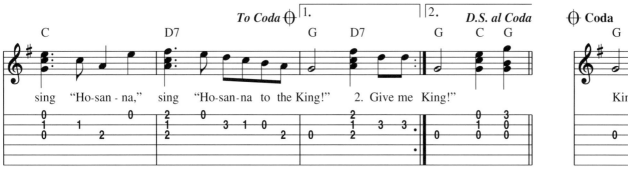

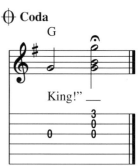

Additional Lyrics

2. Give me oil in my lamp, keep me burning, burning, burning.
Give me oil in my lamp, I pray, Hallelujah!
Oil in my lamp, keep me burning, burning, burning,
Keep me burning till the break of day!

God Is So Good

Traditional

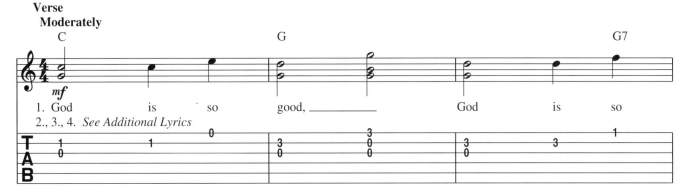

Strum Pattern: 2, 3
Pick Pattern: 2, 4

Verse
Moderately

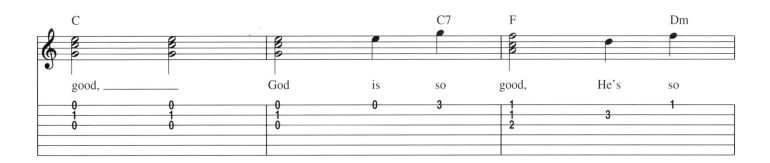

1. God is so good, God is so
2., 3., 4. *See Additional Lyrics*

good, God is so good, He's so

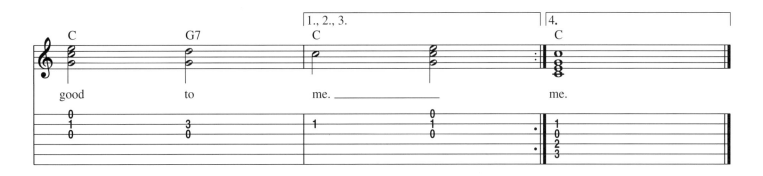

good to me. me.

Additional Lyrics

2. He cares for me, He cares for me,
He cares for me, He's so good to me.

3. He loves me so, He loves me so,
He loves me so, He's so good to me.

4. God is so good, God is so good,
God is so good, He's so good to me.

Hallelu, Hallelujah!

Traditional

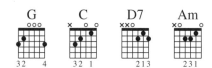

Strum Pattern: 3, 4
Pick Pattern: 3, 5

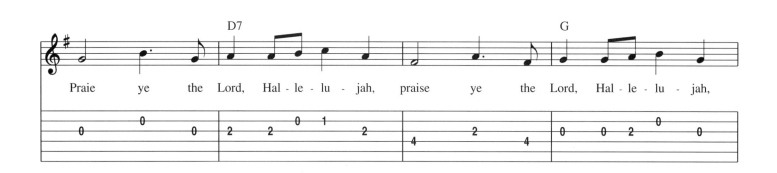

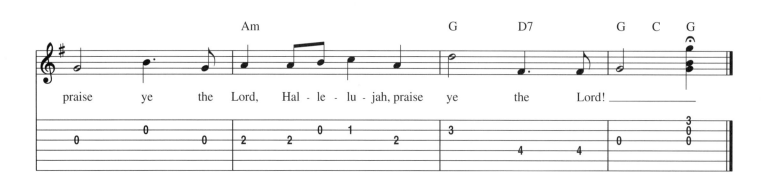

He's Got the Whole World in His Hands

African-American Folksong

Strum Pattern: 3, 4
Pick Pattern: 1, 3

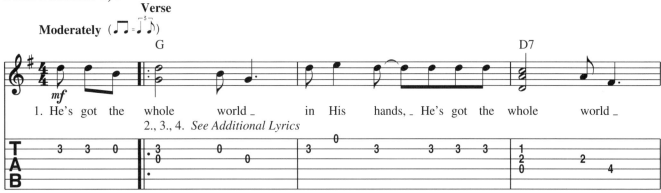

1. He's got the whole world _ in His hands, _ He's got the whole world _
2., 3., 4. *See Additional Lyrics*

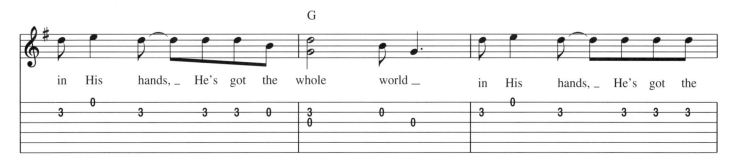

in His hands, _ He's got the whole world _ in His hands, _ He's got the

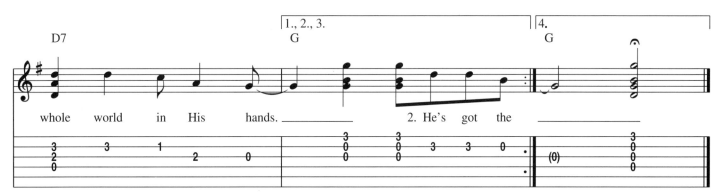

whole world in His hands. _____ 2. He's got the _____

Additional Lyrics

2. He's got the wind and the rain in His hands,
   He's got the wind and the rain in His hands,
   He's got the wind and the rain in His hands,
   He's got the whole world in His hands.

3. He's got the tiny little baby in His hands,
   He's got the tiny little baby in His hands,
   He's got the tiny little baby in His hands,
   He's got the whole world in His hands.

4. He's got you and me, brother, in his hands,
   He's got you and me, sister, in his hands,
   He's got you and me, brother, in his hands,
   He's got the whole world in his hands.

I Am a C-H-R-I-S-T-I-A-N

Traditional

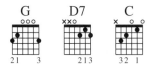

Strum Pattern: 1
Pick Pattern: 2

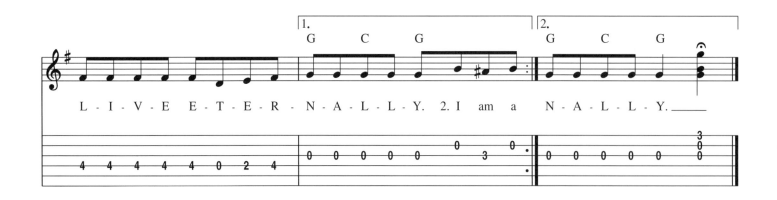

I'll Be a Sunbeam

Words by Nellie Talbot
Music by Edwin O. Excell

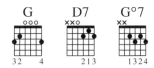

Strum Pattern: 8
Pick Pattern: 8

Verse
Moderately

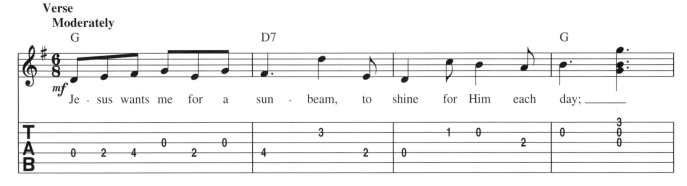

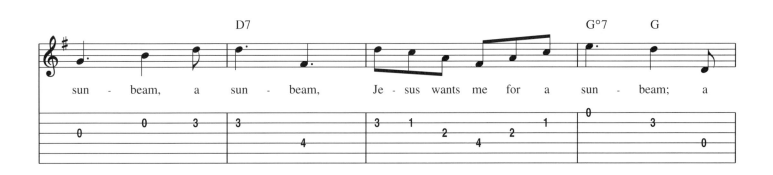

I'm in the Lord's Army

Traditional

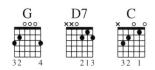

Strum Pattern: 2, 3
Pick Pattern: 2, 3

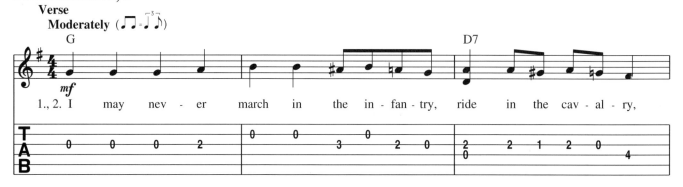

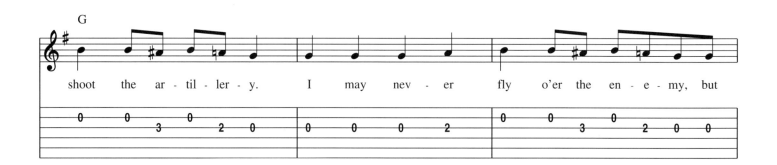

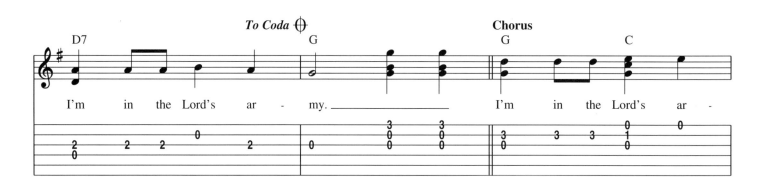

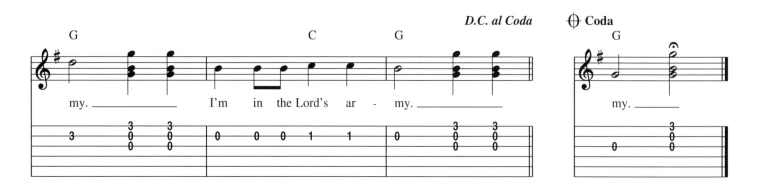

I've Got Peace Like a River

Traditional

Additional Lyrics

2. I've got love like an ocean,
   I've got love like an ocean,
   I've got love like an ocean in my soul.
   I've got love like an ocean,
   I've got love like an ocean,
   I've got love like an ocean in my soul. (My soul.)

3. I've got joy like a fountain,
   I've got joy like a fountain,
   I've got joy like a fountain in my soul.
   I've got joy like a fountain,
   I've got joy like a fountain,
   I've got joy like a fountain in my soul. (My soul.)

If You're Happy and You Know It

Words and Music by L. Smith

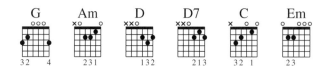

Strum Pattern: 1, 4
Pick Pattern: 2, 5

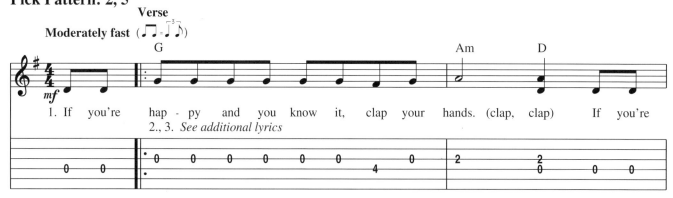

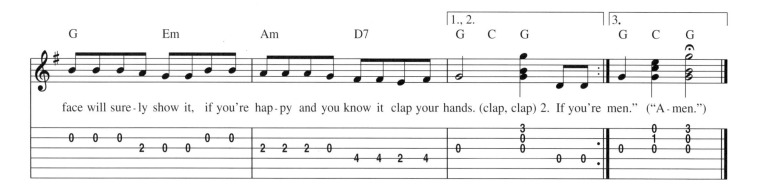

Additional Lyrics

2. If you're happy and you know it, stomp your feet. (stomp, stomp)
   If you're happy and you know it, stomp your feet. (stomp, stomp)
   If you're happy and you know it, then your face will surely show it.
   If you're happy and you know it, stomp your feet. (stomp, stomp)

3. If you're happy and you know it, say "Amen." ("Amen.")
   If you're happy and you know it, say "Amen." ("Amen.")
   If you're happy and you know it, then your face will surely show it.
   If you're happy and you know it, say "Amen." ("Amen.")

Jesus Bids Us Shine

Words by Susan Warner
Music by Edwin Excell

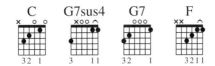

Strum Pattern: 4
Pick Pattern: 1

Verse
Moderately

1. Je - sus bids us shine, with a clear, pure light, like a lit - tle can - dle
2., 3. *See additional lyrics*

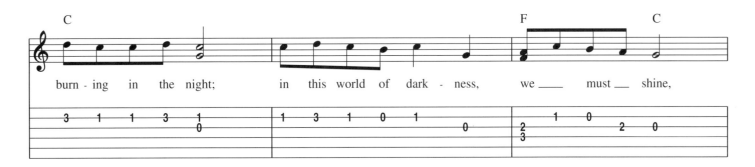

burn - ing in the night; in this world of dark - ness, we ___ must ___ shine,

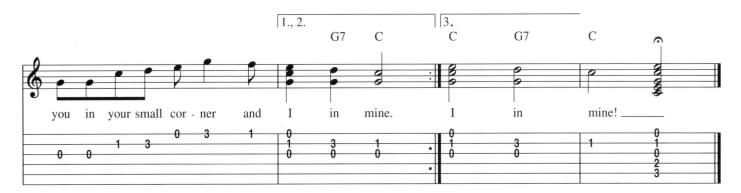

you in your small cor - ner and I in mine. I in mine! ___

Additional Lyrics

2. Jesus bids us shine, first of all for Him.
   Well, He sees and knows it if our light is dim;
   He looks down from heaven, sees us shine,
   You in your small corner and I in mine.

3. Jesus bids us shine as we work for Him,
   Bringing those that wander from paths of sin;
   He will ever help us if we shine,
   You in your small corner and I in mine!

Jacob's Ladder

African-American Spiritual

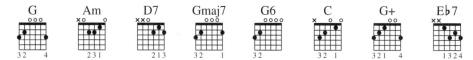

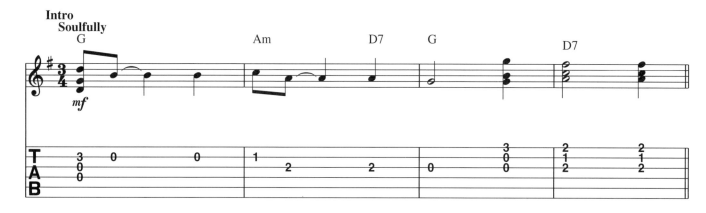

Strum Pattern: 8
Pick Pattern: 8

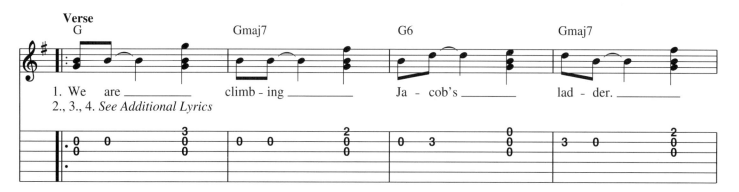

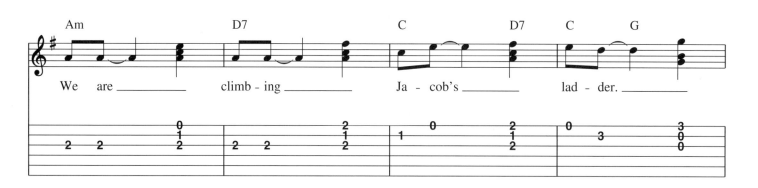

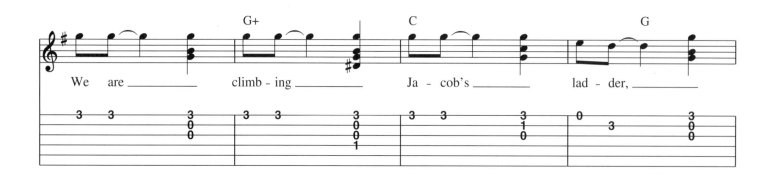

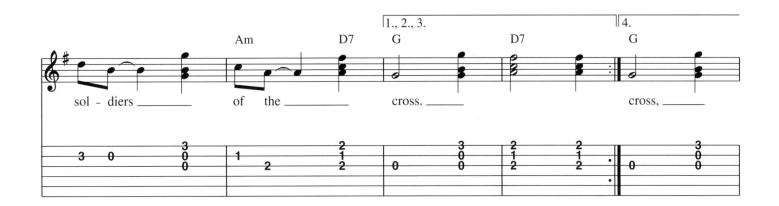

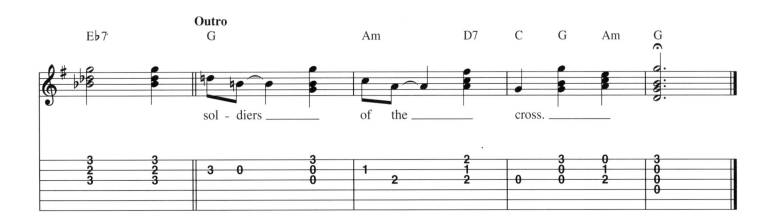

Additional Lyrics

2. Ev'ry round goes higher, higher.
   Ev'ry round goes higher, higher.
   Ev'ry round goes higher, higher,
   Soldiers of the cross.

3. We are climbing higher, higher.
   We are climbing higher, higher.
   We are climbing higher, higher,
   Soldiers of the cross.

4. If you love Him, why not serve Him?
   If you love Him, why not serve Him?
   If you love Him, why not serve Him?
   Soldiers of the cross,

Jesus Loves Even Me
(I Am So Glad)

By P.P. Bliss

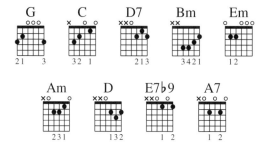

Strum Pattern: 8
Pick Pattern: 8

Chorus
Jazz Waltz

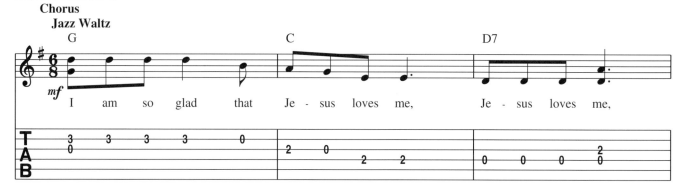

I am so glad that Je - sus loves me, Je - sus loves me,

Je - sus loves me. I am so glad that Je - sus loves me,

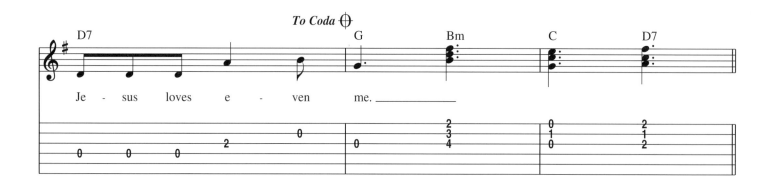

Je - sus loves e - ven me. _____

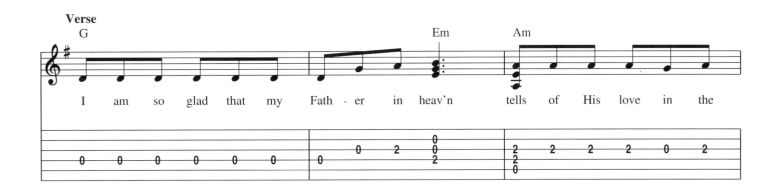

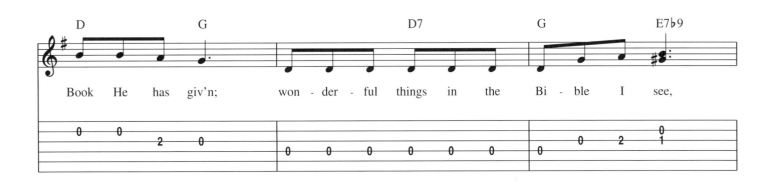

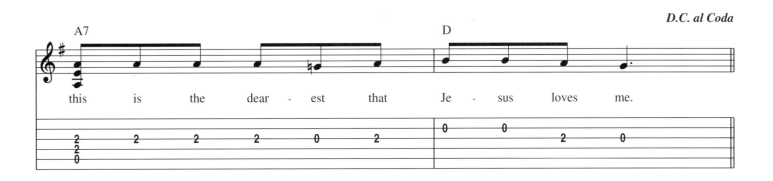

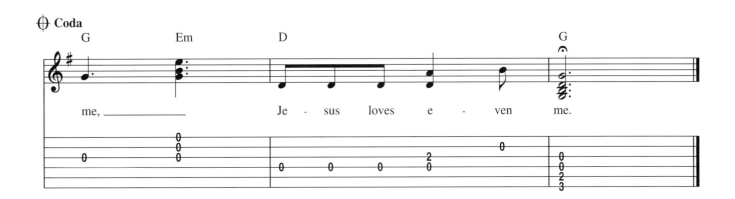

Jesus Loves Me

Words by Anna Warner
Music By William Bradbury

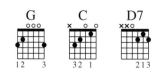

Strum Pattern: 3
Pick Pattern: 3

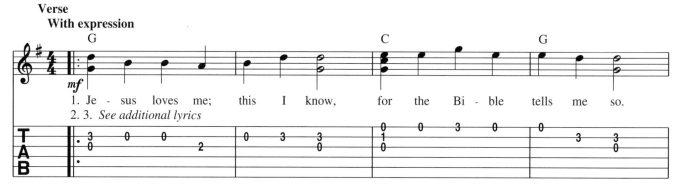

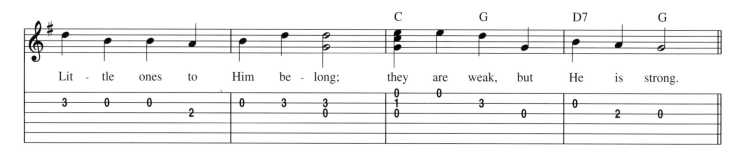

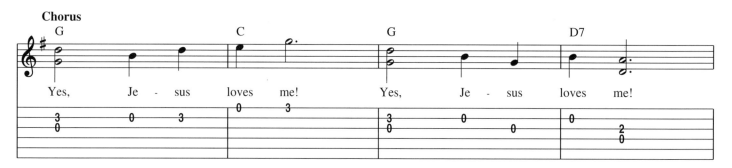

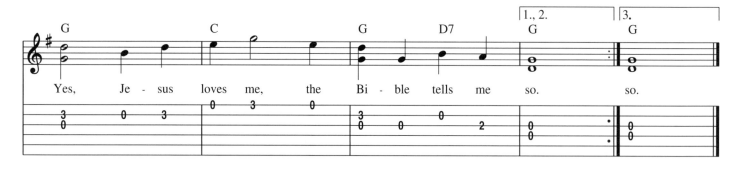

Additional Lyrics

2. Jesus, take this heart of mine,
Make it pure and wholly Thine.
Thou hast bled and died for me,
I will henceforth live for Thee.

3. Jesus loves me; He who died,
Heaven's gate to open wide.
He will wash away my sin,
Let His little child come in.

Jesus Loves the Little Children

Words by Rev. C. H. Woolston
Music by George F. Root

Strum Pattern: 5
Pick Pattern: 4

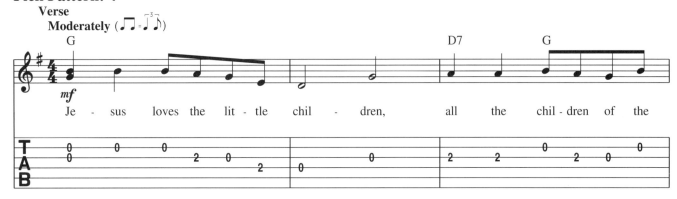

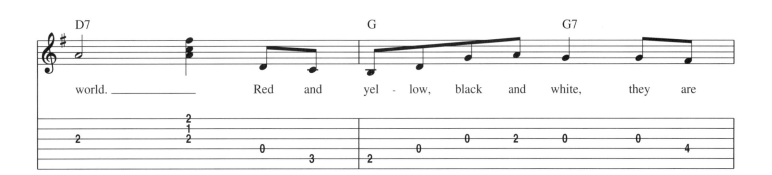

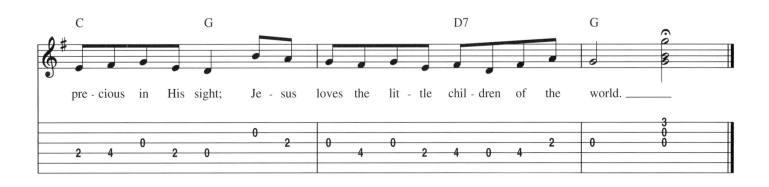

Joshua
(Fit the Battle of Jericho)

African-American Spiritual

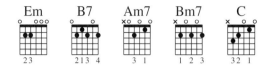

Strum Pattern: 4
Pick Pattern: 1

Chorus
Moderately slow

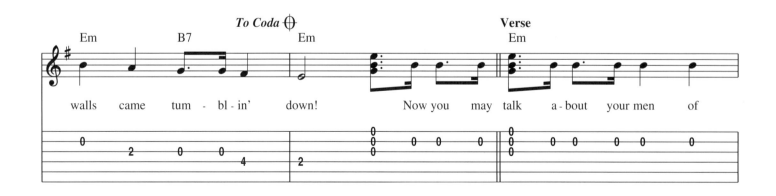

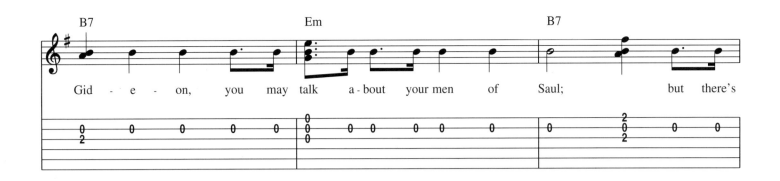

Gid - e - on, you may talk a - bout your men of Saul; but there's

D.C. al Coda

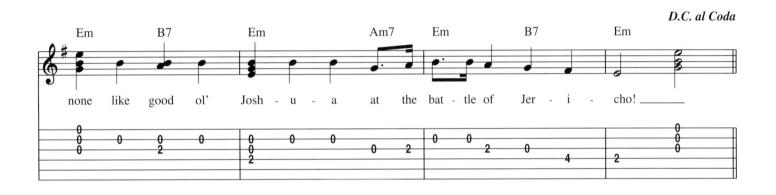

none like good ol' Josh - u - a at the bat - tle of Jer - i - cho! _____

⊕ **Coda**

Outro

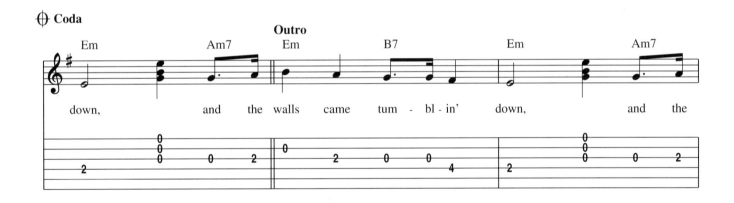

down, and the walls came tum - bl - in' down, and the

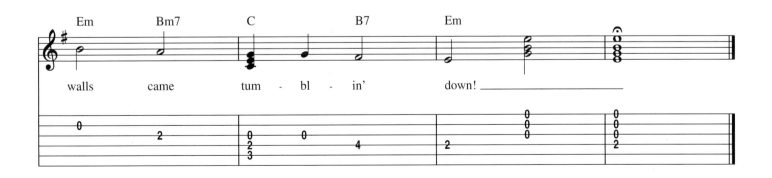

walls came tum - bl - in' down! _____

Kum Ba Yah

Traditional

Strum Pattern: 4
Pick Pattern: 1, 2

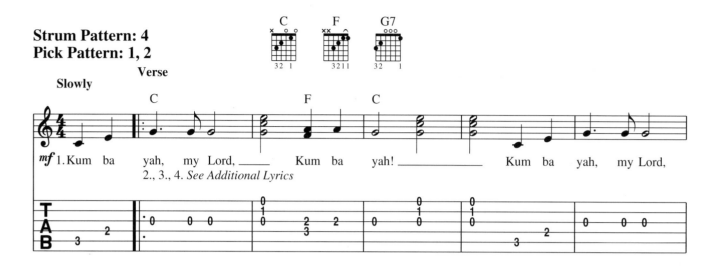

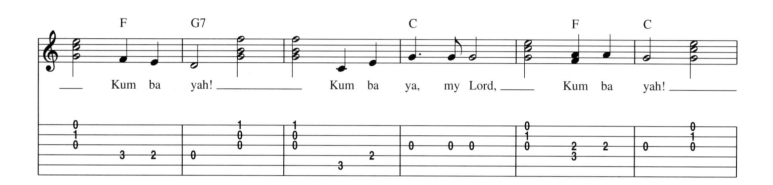

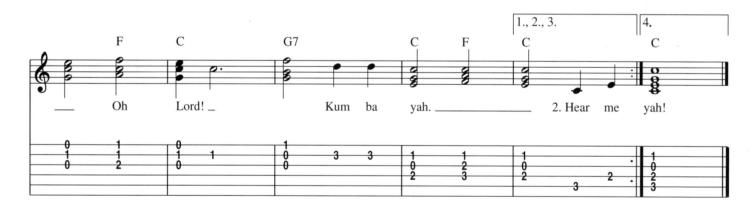

Additional Lyrics

2. Hear me crying, Lord, Kum ba ya!
   Hear me crying, Lord, Kum ba ya!
   Hear me crying, Lord, Kum ba ya!
   Oh Lord! Kum ba ya!

3. Hear me praying, Lord, Kum ba ya!
   Hear me praying, Lord, Kum ba ya!
   Hear me praying, Lord, Kum ba ya!
   O Lord! Kum ba ya!

4. Oh I need you, Lord, Kum ba ya!
   Oh I need you, Lord, Kum ba ya!
   Oh I need you, Lord, Kum ba ya!
   Oh Lord! Kum ba ya!

Lord, I Want to Be a Christian

Traditional Negro Spiritual

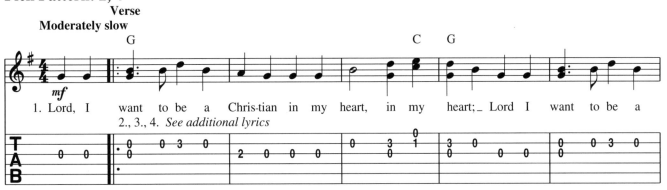

Strum Pattern: 1, 3
Pick Pattern: 2, 4

Verse
Moderately slow

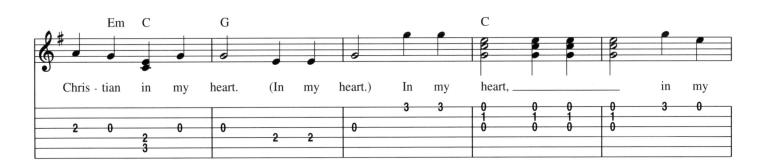

1. Lord, I want to be a Chris-tian in my heart, in my heart;_ Lord I want to be a
2., 3., 4. *See additional lyrics*

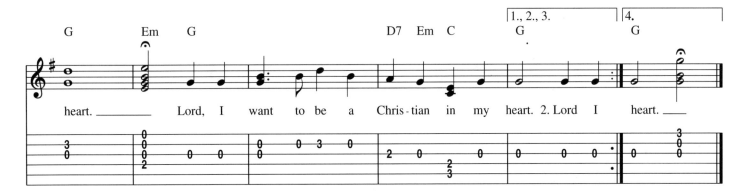

Chris - tian in my heart. (In my heart.) In my heart, ___ in my

heart. ___ Lord, I want to be a Chris - tian in my heart. 2. Lord I heart. ___

Additional Lyrics

2. Lord, I want to be more loving in my heart, in my heart;
   Lord, I want to be more loving in my heart. (In my heart.)
   In my heart, in my heart,
   Lord, I want to be more loving in my heart.

3. Lord, I want to be more holy in my heart, in my heart;
   Lord, I want to be more holy in my heart. (In my heart.)
   In my heart, in my heart,
   Lord, I want to be more holy in my heart.

4. Lord, I want to be like Jesus in my heart, in my heart;
   Lord, I want to be like Jesus in my heart. (In my heart.)
   In my heart, in my heart,
   Lord, I want to be like Jesus in my heart.

Oh, Be Careful

Traditional

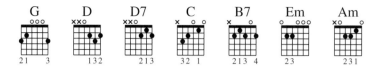

Strum Pattern: 1
Pick Pattern: 2

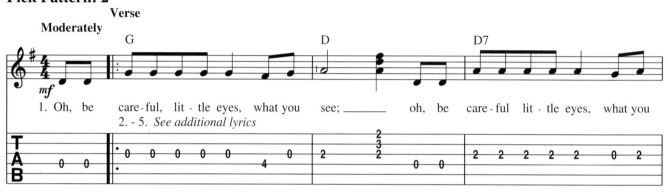

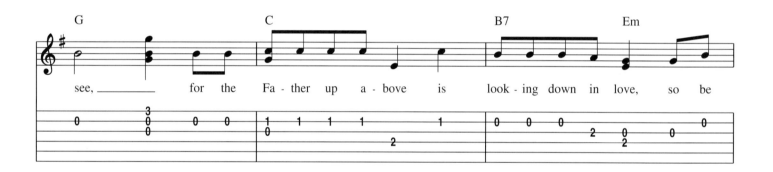

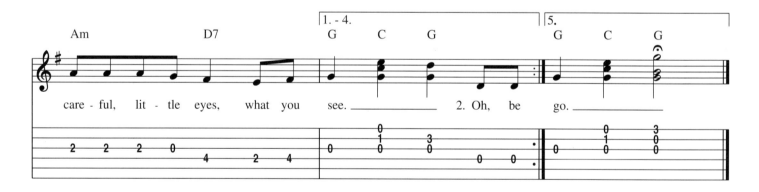

Additional Lyrics

2. Oh, be careful, little ears, what you hear;
   Oh, be careful, little ears, what you hear,
   For the Father up above is looking down in love,
   So be careful, little ears, what you hear.

3. Oh, be careful, little tongue, what you say;
   Oh, be careful, little tongue, what you say,
   For the Father up above is looking down in love,
   So be careful, little tongue, what you say.

4. Oh, be careful, little hands, what you do;
   Oh, be careful, little hands, what you do,
   For the Father up above is looking down in love,
   So be careful, little hands, what you do.

5. Oh, be careful, little feet, where you go;
   Oh, be careful, little feet, where you go,
   For the Father up above is looking down in love,
   So be careful, little feet, where you go.

Oh, How I Love Jesus

Words by Frederick Whitfield
Traditional American Melody

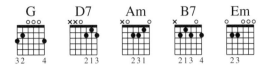

Strum Pattern: 8
Pick Pattern: 8

Verse
Moderately

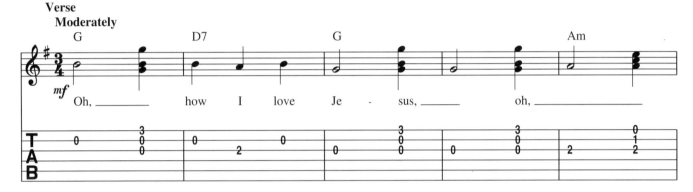

Oh, _____ how I love Je - sus, _____ oh, _____

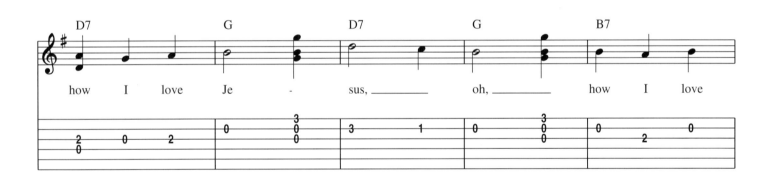

how I love Je - sus, _____ oh, _____ how I love

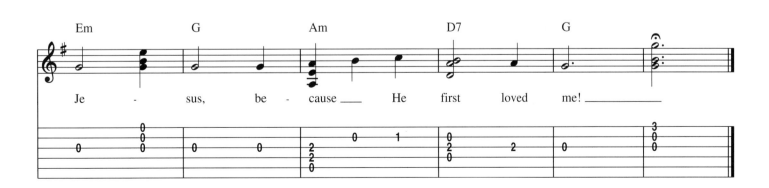

Je - sus, be - cause ____ He first loved me! _____

Praise Him, All Ye Little Children

Anonymous Text
Music by Carey Bonner

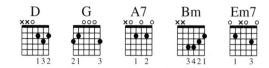

Strum Pattern: 1, 3
Pick Pattern: 2, 4

Verse
Moderately

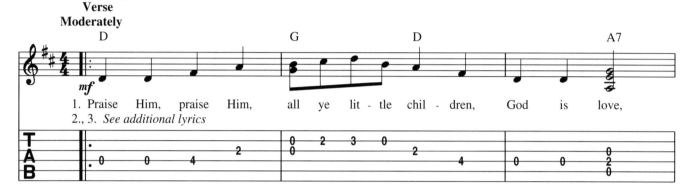

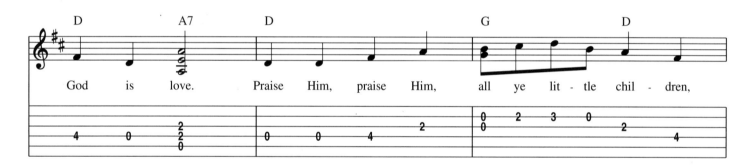

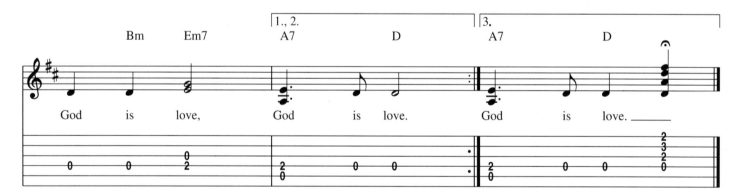

Additional Lyrics

2. Love Him, love Him, all ye little children,
   God is love, God is love.
   Love Him, love Him, all ye little children,
   God is love, God is love.

3. Thank Him, thank Him, all ye little children,
   God is love, God is love.
   Thank Him, thank Him, all ye little children,
   God is love, God is love.

Standin' in the Need of Prayer

African-American Spritual

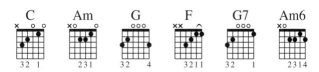

Strum Pattern: 4
Pick Pattern: 1

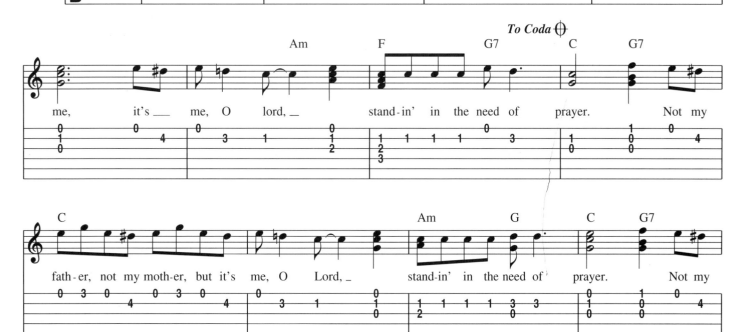

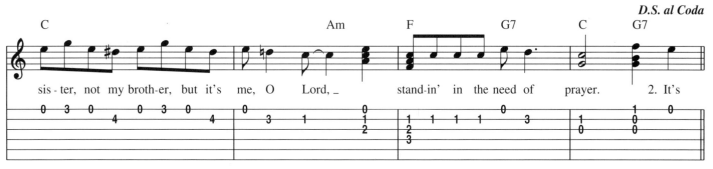

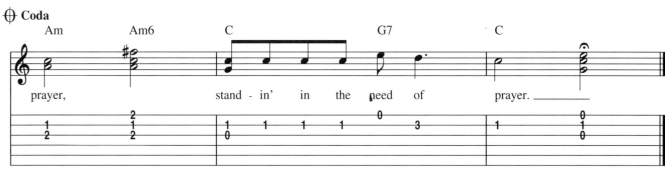

Tell Me the Story of Jesus

Words by Fanny J. Crosby
Music by John R. Sweney

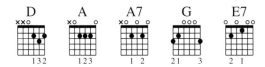

Strum Pattern: 1, 3
Pick Pattern: 2, 4

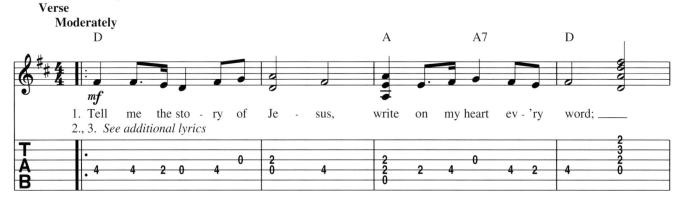

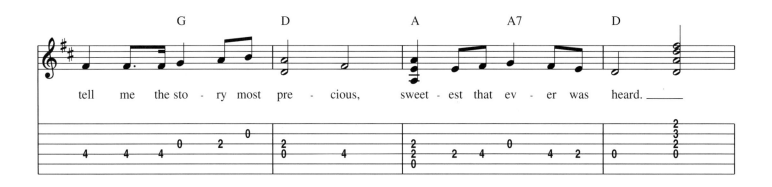

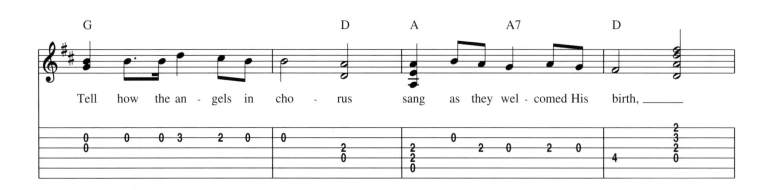

"Glo - ry to God in the high - est! Peace and good ti - dings to earth." _____

Chorus

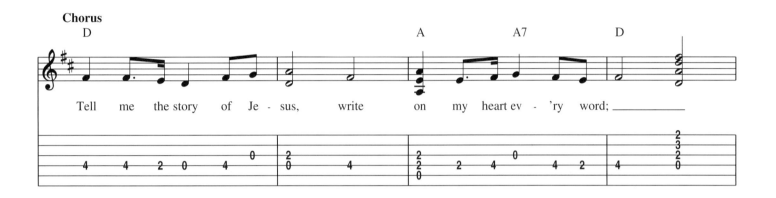

Tell me the story of Je - sus, write on my heart ev - 'ry word; _____

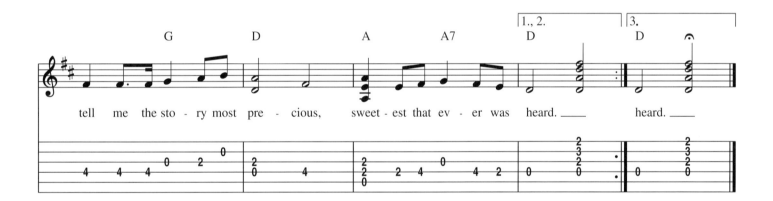

tell me the sto - ry most pre - cious, sweet - est that ev - er was heard. _____ heard. _____

Additional Lyrics

2. Fasting alone in the desert,
   Tell of the days that are past,
   How for our sins He was tempted,
   Yet was triumphant at last.
   Tell of the years of His labor,
   Tell of the sorrow He bore,
   He was despised and afflicted,
   Homeless, rejected and poor.

3. Tell of the cross where they nailed Him,
   Writhing in anguish and pain;
   Tell of the grave where they laid Him,
   Tell how He liveth again.
   Love in that story so tender,
   Clearer than ever I see:
   Stay, let me weep while you whisper,
   Love paid the ransom for me.

This Little Light of Mine

African-American Spiritual

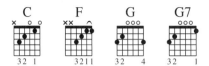

Strum Pattern: 2, 4
Pick Pattern: 5, 4

Chorus
Moderately

This lit - tle light of mine, _____ I'm gon - na let it

shine. _____ This lit - tle light of mine, _____ I'm gon - na let it

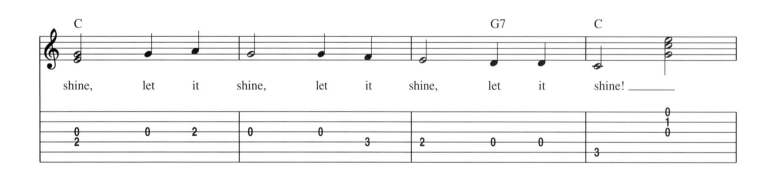

shine, let it shine, let it shine, let it shine! _____

Verse

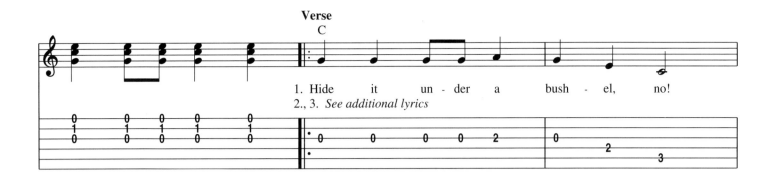

1. Hide it un - der a bush - el, no!
2., 3. *See additional lyrics*

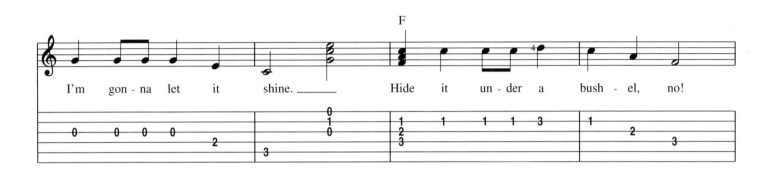

I'm gon - na let it shine. _____ Hide it un - der a bush - el, no!

I'm gon - na let it shine, let it shine, let it shine, let it

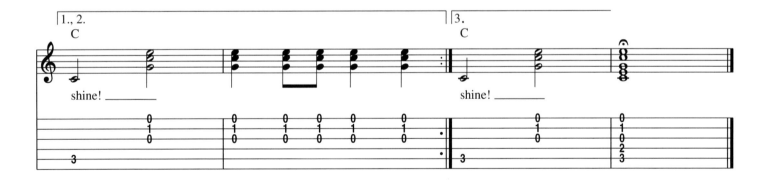

shine! _____ shine! _____

Additional Lyrics

2. Don't let Satan (blow) it out,
   I'm gonna let it shine.
   Don't let Satan (blow) it out,
   I'm gonna let it shine, let it shine,
   Let it shine, let it shine!

3. Let it shine till Jesus comes,
   I'm gonna let it shine.
   Let it shine till Jesus comes,
   I'm gonna let it shine, let it shine,
   Let it shine, let it shine!

This Is My Father's World

Words by Maltbie Babcock
Music by Franklin L. Sheppard

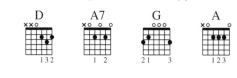

Strum Pattern: 2
Pick Pattern: 2

Additional Lyrics

2. This is my Father's world, the birds their carrols raise.
   The morning light, the lily white, declare their maker's praise.
   This is my Father's world, He shines in all that's fair.
   In the rustling grass I hear Him pass, He speaks to me everywhere.

3. This is my Father's world, oh let me ne'er forget
   That though the wrong seems oft so strong, God is the Ruler yet.
   This is my Father's world, the battle is not done.
   Jesus who died shall be satisfied, and earth and heav'n be one.

When the Saints Go Marching In

Words by Katherine E. Purvis
Music by James M. Black

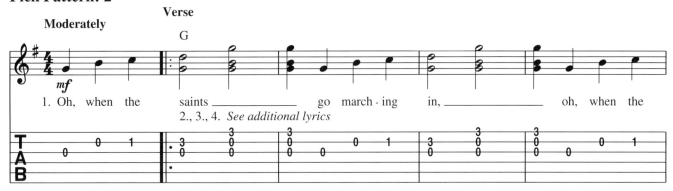

Strum Pattern: 1
Pick Pattern: 2

Moderately

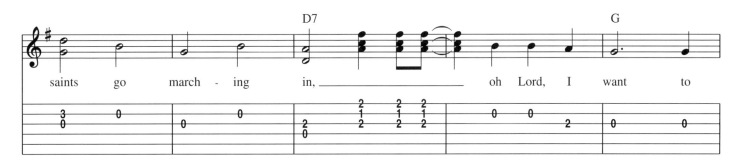

1. Oh, when the saints _____ go march-ing in, _____ oh, when the
2., 3., 4. *See additional lyrics*

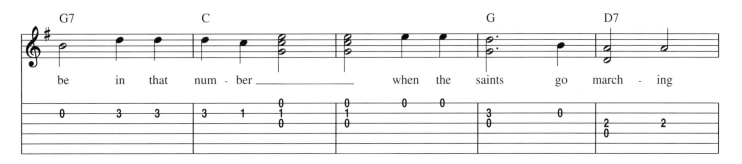

saints go march - ing in, _____ oh Lord, I want to

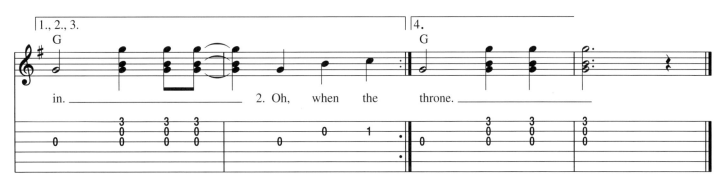

be in that num - ber _____ when the saints go march - ing

1., 2., 3.

in. _____ 2. Oh, when the throne. _____

4.

Additional Lyrics

2. Oh, when the sun refuse to shine,
Oh, when the sun refuse to shine,
Oh Lord, I want to be in that number,
When the sun refuse to shine.

3. Oh, when they crown Him Lord of all,
Oh, when they crown Him Lord of all,
Oh Lord, I want to be in that number,
When they crown Him Lord of all.

4. Oh, when they gather 'round the throne,
Oh, when they gather 'round the throne,
Oh Lord, I want to be in that number,
When they gather 'round the throne.

Zaccheus Was a Wee Little Man

Traditional

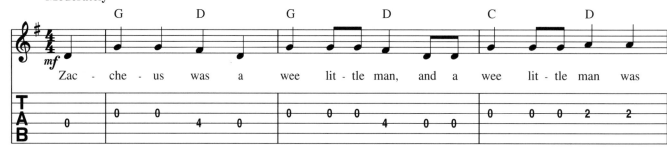

Strum Pattern: 3, 4
Pick Pattern: 3, 5

Verse
Moderately

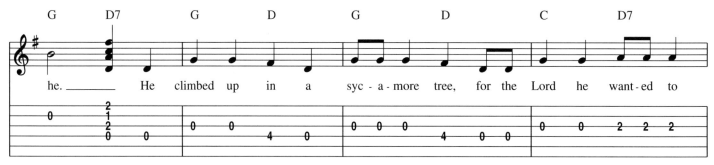

Zac - che - us was a wee lit - tle man, and a wee lit - tle man was

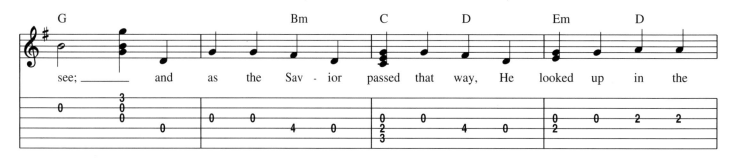

he. _____ He climbed up in a syc - a - more tree, for the Lord he want - ed to

see; _____ and as the Sav - ior passed that way, He looked up in the

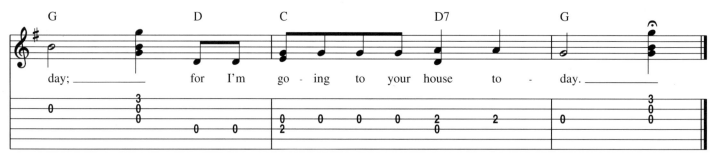

A tempo

tree, _____ *Spoken: And He said, "Zaccheus... you come down!"* For I'm go - ing to your house to -

day; _____ for I'm go - ing to your house to - day. _____

christian guitar songbooks

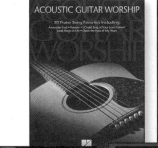

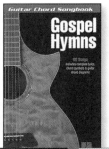

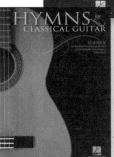

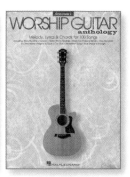

ACOUSTIC GUITAR WORSHIP

30 praise song favorites arranged for guitar, including: Awesome God • Forever • I Could Sing of Your Love Forever • Lord, Reign in Me • Open the Eyes of My Heart • and more.
00699672 Solo Guitar...$14.99

FAVORITE HYMNS FOR SOLO GUITAR

Amazing Grace • Christ the Lord Is Risen Today • For the Beauty of the Earth • Holy, Holy, Holy • In the Garden • Let Us Break Bread Together • O for a Thousand Tongues to Sing • Were You There? • What a Friend We Have in Jesus • When I Survey the Wondrous Cross • more.
00699275 Fingerstyle Guitar $12.99

FINGERPICKING HYMNS

Abide with Me • Amazing Grace • Beneath the Cross of Jesus • Come, Thou Fount of Every Blessing • For the Beauty of the Earth • A Mighty Fortress Is Our God • Rock of Ages • and more.
00699688 Solo Guitar...$9.99

FINGERPICKING WORSHIP

Agnus Dei • Amazing Grace (My Chains Are Gone) • How Deep the Father's Love for Us • How Great Is Our God • I Worship You, Almighty God • More Precious Than Silver • There Is a Redeemer • We Fall Down • and more, plus an easy introduction to basic fingerstyle guitar.
00700554 Solo Guitar...$10.99

GOSPEL GUITAR SONGBOOK

Includes notes & tab for fingerpicking and Travis picking arrangements of 15 favorites: Amazing Grace • Blessed Assurance • Do Lord • I've Got Peace Like a River • Just a Closer Walk with Thee • O Happy Day • Precious Memories • Rock of Ages • Swing Low, Sweet Chariot • There Is Power in the Blood • When the Saints Go Marching In • and more!
00695372 Guitar with Notes & Tab $9.95

GOSPEL HYMNS

Amazing Grace • At the Cross • Blessed Assurance • Higher Ground • I've Got Peace like a River • In the Garden • Love Lifted Me • The Old Rugged Cross • Rock of Ages • What a Friend We Have in Jesus • When the Saints Go Marching In • Wondrous Love • and more.
00700463
Lyrics/Chord Symbols/Guitar Chord Diagrams........$14.99

HYMNS FOR CLASSICAL GUITAR

Amazing Grace • Be Thou My Vision • Come, Thou Fount of Every Blessing • For the Beauty of the Earth • Joyful, Joyful, We Adore Thee • My Faith Looks up to Thee • Rock of Ages • What a Friend We Have in Jesus • and more.
00701898 Solo Guitar...$14.99

HYMNS FOR SOLO JAZZ GUITAR

Book/Online Video

Abide with Me • Amazing Grace • Blessed Assurance • God Is So Good • Just a Closer Walk with Thee • Londonderry Air • Oh How I Love Jesus • Softly and Tenderly • Sweet Hour of Prayer • What a Friend We Have in Jesus.
00153842 Solo Guitar...$19.99

MODERN WORSHIP – GUITAR CHORD SONGBOOK

Amazed • Amazing Grace (My Chains Are Gone) • At the Cross • Beautiful One • Everlasting God • How Can I Keep from Singing • I Am Free • Let God Arise • Let My Words Be Few (I'll Stand in Awe of You) • Made to Worship • Mighty to Save • Nothing but the Blood • Offering • Sing to the King • Today Is the Day • Your Name • and more.
00701801
Lyrics/Chord Symbols/Guitar Chord Diagrams........$16.99

PRAISE & WORSHIP – STRUM & SING

This inspirational collection features 25 favorites for guitarists to strum and sing. Includes chords and lyrics for: Amazing Grace (My Chains Are Gone) • Cornerstone • Everlasting God • Forever • The Heart of Worship • How Great Is Our God • In Christ Alone • Mighty to Save • 10,000 Reasons (Bless the Lord) • This I Believe • We Fall Down • and more.
00152381 Guitar/Vocal $12.99

SACRED SONGS FOR CLASSICAL GUITAR

Bind Us Together • El Shaddai • Here I Am, Lord • His Name Is Wonderful • How Great Thou Art • I Walked Today Where Jesus Walked • On Eagle's Wings • Thou Art Worthy • and more.
00702426 Guitar...$14.99

SUNDAY SOLOS FOR GUITAR

Great Is Thy Faithfulness • Here I Am to Worship • How Great Is Our God • Joyful, Joyful, We Adore Thee • There Is a Redeemer • We Fall Down • What a Friend We Have in Jesus • and more!
00703083 Guitar...$14.99

TOP CHRISTIAN HITS – STRUM & SING GUITAR

Good Good Father (Chris Tomlin) • Greater (MercyMe) • Holy Spirit (Francesca Battistelli) • I Am (Crowder) • Same Power (Jeremy Camp) • This Is Amazing Grace (Phil Wickham) • and more.
00156331 Guitar/Vocal $12.99

THE WORSHIP GUITAR ANTHOLOGY – VOLUME 1

This collection contains melody, lyrics & chords for 100 contemporary favorites, such as: Beautiful One • Forever • Here I Am to Worship • Hosanna (Praise Is Rising) • How He Loves • In Christ Alone • Mighty to Save • Our God • Revelation Song • Your Grace Is Enough • and dozens more.
00101864 Melody/Lyrics/Chords...........................$16.99

WORSHIP SOLOS FOR FINGERSTYLE GUITAR

Ancient Words • Before the Throne of God Above • Broken Vessels (Amazing Grace) • Cornerstone • Good Good Father • Great Are You Lord • Holy Spirit • I Will Rise • King of My Heart • Lord, I Need You • O Come to the Altar • O Praise the Name (Anastasis) • Oceans (Where Feet May Fail) • 10,000 Reasons (Bless the Lord) • Your Name.
00276831 Guitar...$14.99

TOP WORSHIP SONGS FOR GUITAR

Amazing Grace (My Chains Are Gone) • Because He Lives, Amen • Cornerstone • Forever (We Sing Hallelujah) • Good Good Father • Holy Spirit • Jesus Messiah • Lead Me to the Cross • Our God • Revelation Song • This Is Amazing Grace • We Believe • Your Grace Is Enough • and more.
00160854 Melody/Lyrics/Chords...........................$12.99

Prices, contents and availability subject to change without notice.

EASY GUITAR WITH NOTES & TAB

This series features simplified arrangements with notes, tab, chord charts, and strum and pick patterns.

MIXED FOLIOS

00702287 Acoustic	$19.99
00702002 Acoustic Rock Hits for Easy Guitar	$17.99
00702166 All-Time Best Guitar Collection	$29.99
00702232 Best Acoustic Songs for Easy Guitar	$16.99
00119835 Best Children's Songs	$16.99
00703055 The Big Book of Nursery Rhymes & Children's Songs	$16.99
00698978 Big Christmas Collection	$19.99
00702394 Bluegrass Songs for Easy Guitar	$15.99
00289632 Bohemian Rhapsody	$19.99
00703387 Celtic Classics	$16.99
00224808 Chart Hits of 2016-2017	$14.99
00267383 Chart Hits of 2017-2018	$14.99
00334293 Chart Hits of 2019-2020	$16.99
00403479 Chart Hits of 2021-2022	$16.99
00702149 Children's Christian Songbook	$9.99
00702028 Christmas Classics	$9.99
00101779 Christmas Guitar	$16.99
00702141 Classic Rock	$8.95
00159642 Classical Melodies	$12.99
00253933 Disney/Pixar's Coco	$19.99
00702203 CMT's 100 Greatest Country Songs	$34.99
00702283 The Contemporary Christian Collection	$16.99

00196954 Contemporary Disney	$19.99
00702239 Country Classics for Easy Guitar	$24.99
00702257 Easy Acoustic Guitar Songs	$17.99
00702041 Favorite Hymns for Easy Guitar	$12.99
00222701 Folk Pop Songs	$19.99
00126894 Frozen	$14.99
00333922 Frozen 2	$14.99
00702286 Glee	$16.99
00702160 The Great American Country Songbook	$19.99
00702148 Great American Gospel for Guitar	$14.99
00702050 Great Classical Themes for Easy Guitar	$9.99
00148030 Halloween Guitar Songs	$17.99
00702273 Irish Songs	$14.99
00192503 Jazz Classics for Easy Guitar	$16.99
00702275 Jazz Favorites for Easy Guitar	$17.99
00702274 Jazz Standards for Easy Guitar	$19.99
00702162 Jumbo Easy Guitar Songbook	$24.99
00232285 La La Land	$16.99
00702258 Legends of Rock	$14.99
00702189 MTV's 100 Greatest Pop Songs	$34.99
00702272 1950s Rock	$16.99
00702271 1960s Rock	$16.99
00702270 1970s Rock	$24.99
00702269 1980s Rock	$16.99

00702268 1990s Rock	$24.99
00369043 Rock Songs for Kids	$14.99
00109725 Once	$14.99
00702187 Selections from O Brother Where Art Thou?	$19.99
00702178 100 Songs for Kids	$16.99
00702515 Pirates of the Caribbean	$17.99
00702125 Praise and Worship for Guitar	$14.99
00287930 Songs from *A Star Is Born, The Greatest Showman, La La Land,* and More Movie Musicals	$16.99
00702285 Southern Rock Hits	$12.99
00156420 Star Wars Music	$16.99
00121535 30 Easy Celtic Guitar Solos	$16.99
00244654 Top Hits of 2017	$14.99
00283786 Top Hits of 2018	$14.99
00302269 Top Hits of 2019	$14.99
00355779 Top Hits of 2020	$14.99
00374083 Top Hits of 2021	$16.99
00702294 Top Worship Hits	$17.99
00702255 VH1's 100 Greatest Hard Rock Songs	$39.99
00702175 VH1's 100 Greatest Songs of Rock and Roll	$34.99
00702253 Wicked	$12.99

ARTIST COLLECTIONS

00702267 AC/DC for Easy Guitar	$17.99
00156221 Adele – 25	$16.99
00396889 Adele – 30	$19.99
00702040 Best of the Allman Brothers	$16.99
00702865 J.S. Bach for Easy Guitar	$15.99
00702169 Best of The Beach Boys	$16.99
00702292 The Beatles — 1	$22.99
00125796 Best of Chuck Berry	$16.99
00702201 The Essential Black Sabbath	$15.99
00702250 blink-182 — Greatest Hits	$19.99
02501615 Zac Brown Band — The Foundation	$19.99
02501621 Zac Brown Band — You Get What You Give	$16.99
00702043 Best of Johnny Cash	$19.99
00702090 Eric Clapton's Best	$16.99
00702086 Eric Clapton — from the Album Unplugged	$17.99
00702202 The Essential Eric Clapton	$19.99
00702053 Best of Patsy Cline	$17.99
00222697 Very Best of Coldplay – 2nd Edition	$17.99
00702229 The Very Best of Creedence Clearwater Revival	$16.99
00702145 Best of Jim Croce	$16.99
00702278 Crosby, Stills & Nash	$12.99
14042809 Bob Dylan	$15.99
00702276 Fleetwood Mac — Easy Guitar Collection	$17.99
00139462 The Very Best of Grateful Dead	$17.99
00702136 Best of Merle Haggard	$19.99
00702227 Jimi Hendrix — Smash Hits	$19.99
00702288 Best of Hillsong United	$12.99
00702236 Best of Antonio Carlos Jobim	$15.99

00702245 Elton John — Greatest Hits 1970–2002	$19.99
00129855 Jack Johnson	$17.99
00702204 Robert Johnson	$16.99
00702234 Selections from Toby Keith — 35 Biggest Hits	$12.95
00702003 Kiss	$16.99
00702216 Lynyrd Skynyrd	$17.99
00702182 The Essential Bob Marley	$17.99
00146081 Maroon 5	$14.99
00121925 Bruno Mars – Unorthodox Jukebox	$12.99
00702248 Paul McCartney — All the Best	$14.99
00125484 The Best of MercyMe	$12.99
00702209 Steve Miller Band — Young Hearts (Greatest Hits)	$12.95
00124167 Jason Mraz	$15.99
00702096 Best of Nirvana	$17.99
00702211 The Offspring — Greatest Hits	$17.99
00138026 One Direction	$17.99
00702030 Best of Roy Orbison	$17.99
00702144 Best of Ozzy Osbourne	$14.99
00702279 Tom Petty	$17.99
00102911 Pink Floyd	$17.99
00702139 Elvis Country Favorites	$19.99
00702293 The Very Best of Prince	$22.99
00699415 Best of Queen for Guitar	$16.99
00109279 Best of R.E.M.	$14.99
00702208 Red Hot Chili Peppers — Greatest Hits	$19.99
00198960 The Rolling Stones	$17.99
00174793 The Very Best of Santana	$16.99
00702196 Best of Bob Seger	$16.99
00146046 Ed Sheeran	$19.99

00702252 Frank Sinatra — Nothing But the Best	$12.99
00702010 Best of Rod Stewart	$17.99
00702049 Best of George Strait	$17.99
00702259 Taylor Swift for Easy Guitar	$15.99
00359800 Taylor Swift – Easy Guitar Anthology	$24.99
00702260 Taylor Swift — Fearless	$14.99
00139727 Taylor Swift — 1989	$19.99
00115960 Taylor Swift — Red	$16.99
00253667 Taylor Swift — Reputation	$17.99
00702290 Taylor Swift — Speak Now	$16.99
00232849 Chris Tomlin Collection – 2nd Edition	$14.99
00702226 Chris Tomlin — See the Morning	$12.95
00148643 Train	$14.99
00702427 U2 — 18 Singles	$19.99
00702108 Best of Stevie Ray Vaughan	$17.99
00279005 The Who	$14.99
00702123 Best of Hank Williams	$15.99
00194548 Best of John Williams	$14.99
00702228 Neil Young — Greatest Hits	$17.99
00119133 Neil Young — Harvest	$16.99

Prices, contents and availability subject to change without notice.

Visit Hal Leonard online at halleonard.com